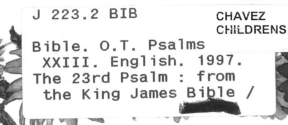

This book belongs to:

_____

To Robin Dailey and family
—M.H.

Henry Holt and Company, Inc.
Publishers since 1866
115 West 18th Street
New York, New York 10011

Henry Holt is a registered trademark of Henry Holt and Company, Inc.

Illustrations copyright © 1999 by Michael Hague
All rights reserved.
Published in Canada by Fitzhenry & Whiteside Ltd.,
195 Allstate Parkway, Markham, Ontario L3R 4T8.

Library of Congress Cataloging-in-Publication Data
Bible. O. T. Psalms XXIII. English.
The 23rd Psalm / illustrated by Michael Hague.
Summary: An illustrated presentation of the Psalm comparing God to a Good Shepherd.
1. Bible O. T. Psalms XXIII—Juvenile literature. [1. Bible. O. T. Psalms XXIII.]
I. Hague, Michael, ill. II. Title.
BS145023rd   1997   223'.2052034—dc20   96-44905

ISBN 0-8050-3820-5 / First Edition—1999
The artist used mixed media on watercolor board to create the illustrations for this book.
Printed in the United States of America on acid-free paper. ∞
1 3 5 7 9 10 8 6 4 2

The 23rd Psalm

From the King James Bible

illustrated by Michael Hague

Henry Holt and Company

NEW YORK

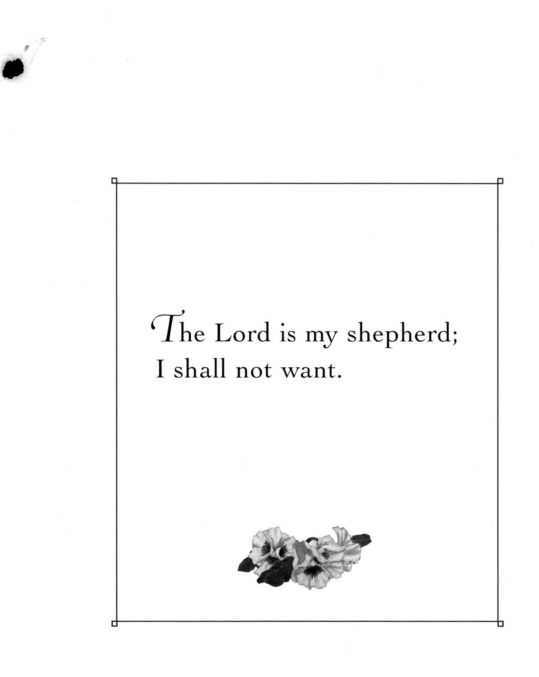

$\mathcal{T}$he Lord is my shepherd;
I shall not want.

He maketh me to lie down
in green pastures:

he leadeth me
beside the still waters.

He restoreth my soul:
he leadeth me in the
paths of righteousness
for his name's sake.

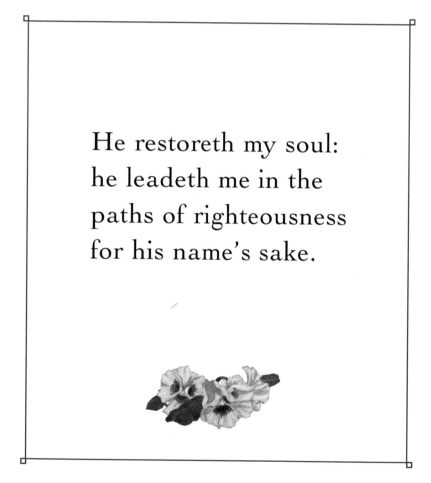

Yea, though I walk
through the valley of
the shadow of death,

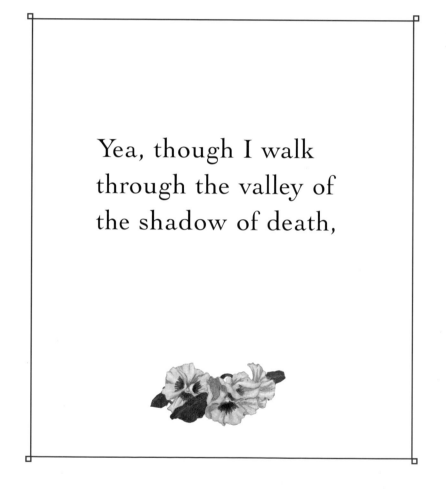

I will fear no evil:
for thou art with me;

thy rod and thy staff
they comfort me.

Thou preparest a table
before me in the presence
of mine enemies:

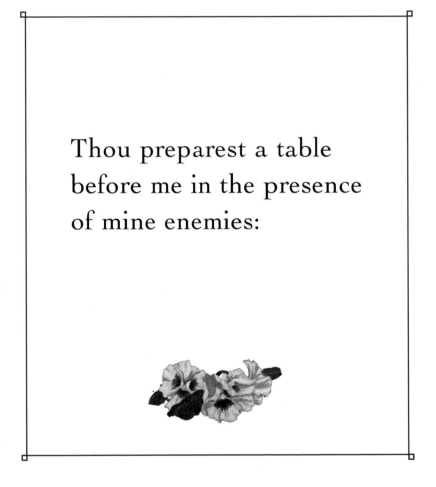

thou anointest
my head with oil;

my cup runneth over.

Surely goodness and
mercy shall follow me
all the days of my life:

and I will dwell
in the house of
the Lord for ever.